# Wasp in My Cockpit

## Derek Dohren

Black Eyes Publishing UK

**Wasp in My Cockpit**
By Derek Dohren
© Derek Dohren, 2020

Published by Black Eyes Publishing UK, 2020
Brockworth, Gloucestershire, England
www.blackeyespublishinguk.co.uk

ISBN:  9781913195137

Derek Dohren has asserted his moral right under the Copyright, Designs and Patents Act, 1988, to be identified as the author of this work.

All Rights reserved.  No part of this publication may be reproduced, copied, stored in a retrieval system, or transmitted, in any form or by any means, without the prior written consent of the copyright holder, nor be otherwise circulated in any form of binding or cover other than that in which it is published and without a similar condition being imposed on the subsequent purchaser.

A CIP catalogue record for this title is available from the British Library.

Front Cover:   Pelágia Pais, Intuitive Guide and Artist
               www.pelagiapais.com

Cover design:  Jason Conway, cre8urbrand.
               www.cre8urbrand.co.uk

Dedicated with love to my girls
Charley and Stacey.

# Wasp in My Cockpit

## Contents

- 7 Introduction
- 11 Notes from a Gloucestershire Orchard
- 12 Lunch Break
- 14 Little Black Dress
- 16 In Plain Sight
- 18 Wasp in My Cockpit
- 20 Unchained
- 21 I've Seen a Swan, but I Cannot Recall the Shape of its Bill with any Degree of Accuracy
- 24 Heart
- 26 The Bottle
- 27 Kimberley
- 28 Drizzle over Hereford
- 31 Goodbye to Summer
- 32 Eleven
- 34 Health Scare
- 37 The 23
- 39 My Heart Will Go On
- 42 Crash
- 44 The Garden of Eden
- 45 I Sometimes Forget
- 46 Dick
- 47 While You Went
- 48 Phil
- 51 Norman and Shirley and Me
- 53 Games Night
- 55 Uncle Mike
- 57 Crouch and Await Your Turn
- 59 Hilton Park Services
- 60 Mighty Silver
- 61 The 13:45
- 63 The Song of the Whale
- 64 Brexit Indifference

65  Listening to Claude Debussy
66  Prick
67  I've Never Been to Bletchley
68  Daisyworld
69  Breakfast at Erol's


73  ...At the embalmed village of St Weonards
75  Derek Dohren
77  Other works by


**Notes**

A version of *Crash* first appeared in *The Cats of the River Darro*, ISBN-13: 978-1478315537, by the same author, in September 2012.

Versions of *Eleven*, *Drizzle Over Hereford* and *Uncle Mike* appear in the Gloucestershire Poetry Society's anthology; *The Trawler 2020*

*Mighty Silver* was first published by the *Lanark Writers* in 2006.

*Goodbye to Summer* was commissioned for and performed on *sonickitchen.fm*, on September 20th 2020.

*Games Night* was first published in *Further Within Darkness and Light*, ISBN-13: 978-1986671675, a poetry collection compiled by Paul B Morris.

# Introduction

Painting remains an important creative outlet for me. The artist's statement that sits on my website begins with "When words are insufficient it is the role of the painter to step in".

On the occasions I turn to the paints and the brushes I am thus relieved of the need to find words to convey a feeling or an experience. Oftentimes this is liberating, but equally so it can lead to a certain dissatisfaction, and the realisation of an unfulfilled vision.

If a picture paints a thousand words then you had better be sure you have precisely transferred the inspirational promptings of your muse onto canvas.

There is no shortage of paint, of colour, of canvas, just as there is no shortage of words in the world. The 26 letters of the alphabet are more than up to the job. The missing ingredient then in whichever of the disciplines I employ may simply be identified as my own technical shortcomings.

On reflection, and with all that in mind, it may be more accurate to amend that artist statement of mine to begin "When one is unable to find the right words …".

Sadly, in such times those paints and brushes may find themselves carrying an unfairly heavy burden of expectation.

But perhaps those deficiencies are really the strengths of the artist, in whichever field of the arts he or she practices. After all, the cracks are where the light gets in.

The world famous classical music composer Claude Debussy was alleged to have remarked that "music is the silence between the notes".

I am always delighted to hear what someone has taken from one of my paintings or poems because the narrative I have arranged may have unlocked a train of thought or teased out a reverberation I had not considered in the creation, irrespective of how successful I felt I had communicated what I had set out to say. This neatly also resolves the 'technical shortcomings' worry. Something has been communicated and received, albeit perhaps 'between the notes', and that's worth celebrating.

I have come to accept there is no separation between my writing and my painting. They are facets of the same thing. The response to a piece of writing or to a painting is at least as important as the motivation behind the creation, at least for this particular artist.

My hope then is that this collection of poetry, my second with Black Eyes Publishing UK, will reveal plenty of shafts of light to illuminate those darker areas.

I wish to thank Josephine and Peter Lay at Black Eyes for the tirelessly professional way they have nudged and cajoled my words into shape and presented them to you in this fine book.

Take the poems however you see fit. Acknowledge the emotions they stir up. Read between the lines. Nod in agreement and rage with indignation.

Enjoy.

Derek Dohren, November 2020

## Notes from a Gloucestershire Orchard

In the lea of May Hill
I see regimented rows of fruit trees
not yet pregnant
'neath a pale blue sky
pimped by contrail slashes
and spiced with butterfly wings.
Mother Nature she
watches me there.

Hunkered down on a fallen log
I watch my cigar smoke curl and melt
over muddy tyre tracks
with their sun-baked crusts
while at my feet
a lone ant busies.
Mother Nature she
watches me there.

## Lunch Break

We sat on park benches
opposite one another
an expanse of neutral grass between us.
You were eating your lunch
and I was eating mine.
Our eyes met briefly
somewhere over that green sea
and I supposed
that if this had been a rom-com
the director would have engineered
a clumsy yet endearing way
in which I could have broken the ice with you.
I wouldn't even have to dream it up.
The scriptwriters would do it for me
and I'd just learn my lines
and sashay on over.
I'd do my pratfall
as I tried to save you
from that seagull
that was trying to eat your
salmon paste sandwiches.

And over the next twenty minutes of screen time
our perfect teeth
and our perfect bodies
would fall in love
and I'd talk passionately about the sun and the moon
and about how they appear to be the same size
in the sky
even though the sun is four hundred times
further away from the earth than the moon is.

But eventually you'd discover my terrible secret
and in my desperate attempts
to redeem myself
I'd haplessly fall victim
to a gross misunderstanding

about your ongoing relationship
with Kevin
before we both finally realized
as we stood soaking wet
on the film studio lot,
the water canon raining down hard on us
that we were made for one another.
And I'd bring that sun and moon thing up again
and say that the moon is four hundred times smaller
than the sun
and that's why they look the same size in the sky
(when it isn't raining).
And that this is either an extremely unlikely coincidence
or it's proof of God's existence.
And you'd press your finger to my lips and say
"It's neither."
Then the director would shout
"It's a wrap!"
And we'd all go home.

You'd go on to make a new film with Brad Pitt
and I'd get some voice over work
for the Gloucestershire County Council, Transport Executive's
future vision video, entitled:
Gloucestershire County Council, Transport Executive - Future
Vision.
But my butties were finished.
So, I stood up
and you pretended to look the other way.
I put the empty wrapper in the bin
and I went back to work.

## Little Black Dress

See her
over there
there
in the shadows
with her best friend
sipping a drink
waiting her turn
at the open mic
as others speak
her body tensed
her mind racing.

See her
sitting there
there
in the shadows
with her best friend
mobile phone to hand
waiting her turn
at the open mic
as others speak
her body tensed
her mind racing.

See her
sipping a drink
mobile phone to hand
in the shadows
with her best friend
in her favourite shoes
waiting her turn
at the open mic
as others speak
she's more than
she thinks she is.

See her
over there
there
waiting her turn
in the shadows
as others speak
she's more than
she thinks she is
she's more
she's much more
than she thinks she is.

See her
standing there
there
her body racing
her mind poised
at the open mic
speaking her truth
from the shadows
listen to her words
she's more than
she thinks she is.

Listen to her
at the open mic
speaking her truth
from the shadows
she's more than
she thinks she is
listen to her words
she's more than
she knows she is
she's much more
than she knows she is.

# In Plain Sight

At home I try to watch
my houseplants photosynthesise
but the process remains hidden
in plain sight.
Instead I'm left snacking at the womb
of the unknown mummy
with one hand rammed up inside
a malicious ventriloquist dummy.

The frilly shirts don't fit any more
and the death of an old unromantic New Romantic
inches nearer.
It's clear to see
I'm not as witty a man as Oscar Wilde
and I don't lead the privileged life
of a Rothschild child.

They've paved the parking lot
and put up a paradise.
Up ahead there's been
some kind of accident
and the traffic is backing up.
I'm barely moving quicker than
the speed of continental drift.
At the current rate of progress
I calculate
it will take
twelve and half million years
before I'm finally
drawn into the subduction zone
of Gloucester Transport Hub;
and I need a pee.

At home I try to watch
the rug creep across the floor
but the process remains hidden
in plain sight.

Instead I have an application form to deal with
but I don't know
if I'm supposed to fill the thing in
or fill the thing out.

The Dalai Lama lives in a rabbit hutch
and the death of an old unholy, new Holiness
inches nearer.
It's clear to see
he's not as revered a man as Nelson Mandela
and he doesn't have the wealth
of a Rockerfeller fella.

## Wasp in My Cockpit

There's a feisty wasp in my cockpit.
It flew in through a barely open window
but is unable to find its way out
even though the window is now fully open.
A passenger gets on at Mitcheldean
and alerts me to a woman over the road
who is trying to get rid of a crow
that's been following her all morning.
"Do you know my mate, Bob?" he asks.
"He drives a bus, in Cornwall."
I toy with telling him I do know Bob
but instead I tell him I don't.
He seems disappointed.
"Well, he works for Stagecoach" he adds.
I glance at the woman over the road.
She does indeed seem to be receiving
unwanted attention from a crow
and is trying to shoo it away
and I think
"What would Jesus do?"
My mind drifts to that weird creature I saw
wriggling and writhing on the surface of a pond
in Newent.

I laugh and I wonder what the hell
is going through the crow's mind.
I head for Gloucester
a thousand concerns now rattling my brain
not least of them is the wasp
but also a very real dread
that on my break I'll get caught up
in one of those awful flash mob things.
It's only a matter of time.
Already this year I've been called *Martin*
by a stranger in a coffee shop
and I've demolished a bus shelter
the one that's right outside my flat, or rather

the one that used to be right outside my flat
until the council scooped it up and took it away.
I spoke at length to a therapist about it all
and spent 40 minutes listening to his woes.
What a waste of my fucking time that was.
What would Jesus have done?
He'd have disappeared for three days
and pretended he was dead
but I don't have the requisite skills.

At Gloucester the feisty wasp alighted.
Thankfully there was no flash mob
so things were seriously looking up.
Later that day I saw an old man
walking up Winter Gate Road
with a spring in his step
enjoying the summer evening
in this the autumn of his life.
Too many odd things like that happen
and I think I've experienced enough synchronicities
to suggest that Cornwall
would be a great place to visit.
If I do go I bet I'll bump into Bob and he'll ask me
if I've ever driven through Mitcheldean
as there's a woman there
who gets followed by a crow.
What would Jesus do?
Well if I had his way with words
I'd relate to Bob a profound parable
involving strange creatures that
wriggle and writhe on the surfaces of ponds
in Newent.

## Unchained

Set free by a throwaway line,
a harsh wind blowing away
the obstruction.

Words of anger and frustration,
now the glimmering shaft of
a guiding light.

Able to live once more, unchained,
life presenting me colours
of the rainbow.

## I've Seen a Swan, but I Cannot Recall the Shape of its Bill with any Degree of Accuracy

When I was last here
I found myself in the park
drawn to the boating lake
you used to take me to
when I was a kid.
It was derelict for years,
vandalised and unloved.
But you'd have been impressed.
The council have cleaned it up
and they want the swans to come back.
Remember how I used to get those
irrational urges
to hold one around the neck
just to see what it would feel like.

You once said to me
swans were a miracle of Nature
and you could never work them out.
But I always took the natural world
at face value.
I was more flummoxed
by the science and mechanics
of things;
like how a diamond stylus
running across the surface
of a rotating vinyl disc
could fill the air
with the God-awful music
you sometimes played!

I later understood
that miracles
are about timing
and are all ascribed as thus
only after being filtered through
a subjective analysis

which itself has been shaped
by cultural prejudices.
I have to say my judgement
hasn't always served me well.
You wouldn't be surprised to know
that I grew up
to be my own worst enemy.
And such a snob at times!

There was that girl I really liked
the one who worked
in the menswear department at Debenhams.
But I could never have imagined
being with a woman
who would be happy to be seen
with a man who bought his clothes
in the menswear department at Debenhams.
I only ever went in
for socks and underpants
but on that fateful day
I also bought
a swan's head walking stick
for your birthday.

The hospital said you were dead
before you hit the floor
and I have clung to that
because it absolves me
of a guilt
I am unable to carry.
When you needed my help
I simply prayed for a miracle
but where's a miracle
when the time's not right?
I never touched
that walking stick again.
My hand around the neck
would never have felt right.

Tomorrow I'll walk around
the boating lake once more,
the one you used to take me to
when I was a kid.
It was derelict for years,
vandalised and unloved.
You'd be impressed, Dad.
The council have cleaned it up
and they want the swans to come back.
You know it's a funny thing that,
I've seen a swan
but I cannot recall
the shape of its bill
with any degree of accuracy.

## Heart

April is here and so is spring
and so is Easter
and so is the first day after
the last day of my previous life.
Where I go from here
is entirely up to me.

Yeah, it's a bit of a struggle to write today.
The words haven't really flowed up to this point
but it's starting to get better now
and I have to say
though writer's block's a bit of a bastard
I always try to stare it down.

My car needs a service.
The bread's gone mouldy.
I think I've got an incurable disease.
I don't remember getting up this morning.
You look like an angel
but I don't tell you.

I fear I'm just filling in
spaces on the paper
with curly blue lines from my ballpoint pen
and that just doesn't really count
because it's a cop out isn't it?

Ooh look at me I've written 300 words
of absolute nothingness.
The rubbish needs recycling.
I haven't got any milk.
I think I need a shave today.
No, don't put that down.

I wish I could write about something profound.
Bananas, chairs, microwave ovens
swinging from the chandelier.

My oldest relative died last week.
I never got around to asking her
about my dad.

But I need to keep moving the pen
because the writing has stopped flowing again.
So, I'll try and kick it off by writing
about how it's stopped flowing
because that sometimes works
but not on this occasion.

I fear I'm just filling in
spaces on the paper
with curly blue lines from my ballpoint pen
and that just doesn't really count
because it's a cop out isn't it?

## The Bottle

An early evening sun
sinks low.
Down the Gloucester Road
an empty plastic bottle
rolls and tumbles.
I steer satisfyingly over it
my wheels astride.
In the wing mirrors
a receding view
of the empty vessel
jerking pugnaciously at
the next advancing vehicle.

The next evening
swings low.
Down the Gloucester Road
the same plastic bottle
nestles at the kerb.
I smile as I drive by it
winking back at me,
in the wing mirrors,
environmentally unfriendly
beautiful and unfazed
scattering the rays
of the early evening sun.

## Kimberley

You're a makeshift misfit, a shipshape sheikh
a shapeshifting, polystyrene paperweight.

You only accept that for which you see evidence
yet everybody knows the best way
to get a Taurus to do something
is to cuddle them and offer them a snack.
Please leave me your comments
in the box provided.

I hear thunderclaps
though there's no hint of any rain
just the taste of sweet intoxication
as you slowly go insane
but life's complications have simplified me
I'm happiest now with a mug
of dandelion tea.

You're a dumbstruck junkie, a punch-drunk punk
a dump-trucking, inflatable clusterfuck.

You only accept that for which you see evidence
yet you believe there is no God
even though there is no evidence
of God's non-existence.
Please stay on the line
your call is important to me.

You're a predicament predicted
in an episode of The Simpsons
from nineteen ninety-three
and by a Nostradamus quatrain
that only made sense to me
when I sat and viewed it
retrospectively.

## Drizzle over Hereford

Light drizzle falls
from a sky, tar macadam grey,
as I advance up the A466.
At the embalmed village of St Weonards
a wooden road sign informs
and I make mental notes:
234 miles to Lands End
six twenty-nine John O'Groats.

Through Wormelow and Callow
closing in on Hereford now;
this drizzle drenched drive.
Picking up speed on the A49
I finally arrive.
On the Ross Road
a pre-pubescent boy
out playing on his bike

gives me a wanker sign.
I feel affronted
until I remember
that my generation will hand over
a completely fucked up planet
to his generation
and I think
"Yeah ok then, fair enough."

It continues to drizzle lightly
as I cruise over the Old Bridge
but I cannot quite find
the right frequency of swipe
for my windscreen wipers
and I don't know what to do.
They are either sweeping too much
or the swipes are too few.

Then I see him on the corner
of Saint Martins and Wye
breaking cover momentarily
from the fancy-dress shop doorway
where he'd sheltered, unironically;
*Bus Spotter Man,*
his plumage adapted to the season
pallid and wan.

His cavernous winter coat designed
to conceal flasks of Bovril
and packets of Dundee cake.
I skirt carefully by
but out shoots a telescopic lens
a coordinated flurry of arms and fingers
and I know I'm snapped
as a fly by a frog.

Before he slinks back to the concrete
I sneak a second glance.
Cowboy boots upon his feet
torn and shredded pants.
I've not seen this one before
probably blown off course by the weather
so I make a new entry and tick him off
in my notebook.

And still the drizzle falls.
At the station animated football fans
congregate menacingly.
Stockport County are in town
and hooded youths take turns
to goad one another
while disinterested police officers
stare at their mobile phones.

I offer up a fervent plea,
"Please don't any of you
even think about getting on."

The second I am able
I pull the bus away
devoid of passengers
through the clag filled traffic spray
to make my way to Monmouth.

I trade waves with a fellow driver
acknowledging the camaraderie
of the shared experience
though my bus is bigger than his
and this makes me feel superior
but only for the briefest of moments
before it makes me feel foolish.
On the Ross Road

I see *Wanker Boy* again
still out with his mates
playing on his bike.
They don't seem to care
what the weather's like
and I want to tell them,
"those friendships forged
when you're only ten,

you're unlikely to ever see
the like of them again."
And at last the weather concurs
that enough is surely enough
and thus, the change occurs.
I'm in the A49 bus lane
when drizzle finally turns
into cathartic full-blown rain.

## Goodbye to Summer

As a nascent daybreak
gave birth to morning
there I was
a child sitting in a corner
learning that one thing
leads to everything.
Oh yeah!

I was gonna have to fake it
before I could ever hope to make it.

So, goodbye to summer.
I guess I missed the meteor shower
and crop circle season passed me by.
Autumn's ink signs the skies
and the rain falls spitefully now
but I know
everything is neutral
except perception.

As a mellowed afternoon
gives birth to evening
here I am
a man standing on a corner
learning that everything
leads to one thing.
Oh yeah!

I know I have to make it
because I can never hope to fake it.

# Eleven

Tossed from the Tower of Babel
in statuesque silence
I lay there unobserved
in splendid splendour,
a flown-out reverie
ampersand, underscore, asterisk
dot com.

Impressing the ladies
with my street magic
it seems there are some things
I can do that God can't.
I don't require
anyone on their knees
praising me for all eternity
for example.
But I was thinking more about
failing and lying
and coming in at number eleven
in someone's all-time top ten list.

Lost at the Battle of Culloden
not a hint of motion
I lay there unobserved
in flagrant vagrancy,
a grown-out topiary
ampersand, underscore, asterisk
dot com.

The prophetic Messiah,
a lingering trespasser,
it seems there are some things
I can do that God can't.
I don't require
anyone on their knees
confessing to me their guilt
for example.

But I was thinking more about
sinning and dying
and coming in at number eleven
in someone's all-time top ten list.

## Health Scare

I'm dying, and so are you.
I need to move this
from a knowing to a feeling,
from my brain to my heart.
Health scare
death stare
born, dead, resurrected,
born again, dead again,
reincarnated.
You're living
you're dying
and so am I.

Why is it only when a doctor
with a clipboard
takes me into that side room
and tells me I've got
just six months left,
perhaps nine,
if the treatment kicks in,
that the penny
will properly drop?

Of course
I could get hit by a bus tomorrow
and, if you live in the Forest of Dean
so could you, too
as I'll be coming through
on the number twenty-two
and I'm not the best bus driver
in the world,
if truth be told.
I've a chequered career
at careering off the road.
So, best stay at home then
though you're more likely to meet
grief there

than if you're out on the street,
in which case you're damned if you do
and you're damned if you don't.
Basically, just damned.

Statistically speaking
if this poem has ever been published
you're reading this
long after I've perished.
And, if it's any sort of comfort,
I was pretty shit
at most things in life,
so, if I can do death
then you can do it too;
it's not the be all and end all
you think it is.
Any fool can do it
even the least amongst us
will achieve it.
I'll munch my heavenly popcorn
as I sit and wait with you
if you want me to
because I'm an old hand at this.

Oh yeah, I'm an old hand at this.

I went and turned a funny hue
last time the Grim Reaper came a reaping.
Deader than John Cleese's *Norwegian Blue*
not pining for the fjords, not sleeping.

But I suppose I'm getting ahead of myself
at the time of writing
I'm not quite dead yet
just dying,

and so are you.
I need to move this
from a knowing to a feeling

from my brain to my heart.
Health scare
death stare
born, dead, resurrected,
born again, dead again,
reincarnated.
You're living
you're dying
and so am I.

# The 23

A school-day morning
hard wet ice
hippopotamus grey
I know exactly where I'm at.
'Welcome to Newnham' the sign says
Thank you for not driving like a prat.
I'm on the 23.
I'll soon be in Blakeney;
views down the Severn estuary
if the boy racers don't take me.

I trundle into the village
of Bream
where sadly, everything
is just as it seems.
Toni the barber
(that's Toni with an 'i')
is on his morning shift
'no appointments necessary'
while next door Sally the florist
offers anniversary gifts.

I accelerate back up
the A48.
'47 casualties in three years,'
a sign appears to proudly boast.
Why not have one while you're here?
No thanks, forgive me if I don't.
Finally, the sun peeks through
and now there's a thaw on.
Westbury-on-Severn thanks you
for not driving like a moron.

And back at the station
I celebrate survival
as I head for my favourite café.

An earnest young man clutching a bible
asks me if I know God
and I say,
"I'm sorry, I need a piss."
I'm irritated by the thought
that apparently, it's now compulsory
for postmen to wear shorts
even though it's fucking January.

A seagull the size
of the national debt
makes that noise seagulls make
and I deliver a cheery epithet.
"Welcome to Gloucester
thank you for not shitting on the pavement."
I'm on the 132 next
I'll be heading for Dymock
where you are thanked most kindly
for not driving like a pillock.

## My Heart Will Go On

Outside Queenie Duvall's pub
hangs a sign
with a ridiculously elaborate,
cursive font design
which urges punters to
*Celebrate & Dine*
and from a distance
I misread it as

'Celine Dion'
My first thought is simply
"Why the fuck is Celine Dion
coming to Cinderford?"
Yet, momentarily I find
my heart is lifted
and a jolt of happiness
shoots me through.

I'm not a particular fan of the
French-Canadian songstress
but nor do I
hold anything against her
and the notion
that such a global megastar
has made room for a slot
on a forthcoming world tour

for a boozer
in the Forest of Dean
lifts my spirits hugely.
Kudos to Queenie
and her clientele.
Celine is coming to Cinderford!
But I read the sign again;
and she isn't.

The estate agent's up for sale.
The charity shop needs a bailout.
The schools are out
and the hospitals are sick.
The country's being carved up
and asset stripped.
Every man and his labradoodle
wants a piece of it

while the politicians
keep on keeping
the politics out of it.
And on the radio
they're interviewing Geoffrey,
an international banker.
Thanks for all the austerity then
Geoff, you chinless wanker.

A deflated inflatable Santa
clings to the broken guttering
the forgotten relic
of a Christmas gone
his sack of gifts
and tidings of goodwill
long since punctured
by the winter chill.

Inside the pub Ms Duvall
pours a scotch on the rocks
and surveys empty tables.
No one is dining.
No one is celebrating
for no one feels able.
She raises her glass
to absent friends.

"To those of us who are
the wrong type of passenger."

Then she crunches the ice
in silent defiance
but another Titanic will sink
into unseen oblivion
and with no help forthcoming
from Celine Dion.

## Crash

One of my cultural reference points of the 1980s is The Smiths' song *Reel Around the Fountain*. That's what was playing on the car radio when me and my mate Ken crashed on the M62. We were on our way back to Liverpool from the 1984 League Cup Final.

Even now, I can't have a car crash without thinking about that song.

We'd beaten Everton 1:0. Graeme Souness scored. Ken's dad, Eddie came out to pick us up. He was a Bluenose. We were a pair of gobby Red Shite. The last thing in the world he wanted to see.

Even now I can't see Graeme Souness on the telly without thinking about Eddie.

I'd damaged my glasses in the impact, just when Morrisey sang about falling out of bed twice. Shit happens. Sadly, there's usually someone worse off. I needed new specs anyway.

Even now I can't fall out of bed without thinking about being pinned and mounted like a butterfly.

I ran across the carriageway and tried to pull a guy out of his wrecked car. He was one of those worse off people. He was caked in blood and he asked me to stop pulling because it hurt too much. Give him his due, he laughed about writing off the wife's car. He was a Red and she was a Blue. A mixed marriage. She was gonna be livid when she found out. She'd say he wrecked her car then died on purpose.

Even now I can't think about dying without thinking about not being able to not die.

Morrisey was callously oblivious and he'd bank his royalty cheque one day. The rest of the Smiths were in this too. I don't imagine they gave a single thought for poor Eddie's plight. Or the bloke in the wrecked car. Or the bloke's bereaved wife.

Even now I can't bank royalty cheques without remaining callously oblivious too.

They built an Ikea superstore at the spot where we crashed. I went back once and there was no plaque, no acknowledgement. It's as if *Reel Around the Fountain* had never been written. Perhaps if we'd crashed to *Heaven Knows I'm Miserable Now* things would've been different?

Even now I can't visit Ikea without thinking about how miserable I am.

But life goes on. I left the M62 behind and I took to wearing contact lenses. I moved to Scotland and began crashing my car on the M8, near the gasworks. 'Glasgow's Miles Better' a sign there proclaimed. No, it fucking wasn't. I crashed twice in two days, in the exact same place. In fairness to them, The Smiths had no hand in either incident.

Even now I can't turn the gas on without thinking about the M8.

If we ever play Everton in a League Cup final again it'll throw up old memories, rip open the scars. These days I listen to new music on Spotify but bands never sing about fountains, none of 'em.

Even now, I can't reel around a fountain without opening up old wounds.


*Bluenose – Everton Supporter*
*Red shite – Liverpool supporter(s)*

## The Garden of Eden

I was moved to tears
by news of your untimely life.
I remember the day we strolled
hand in hand
through Elgar country
or somewhere
and I pointed out the tree canopies
and their crown shyness.
"Seasonal fluctuations", you said.
"Enigma Variations", I said.
A lone oak sowing its seeds.
Your steadfast love, Oh Lord,
extends to the heavens
but even The Garden of Eden has weeds.

I asked a simple question
inviting a single sentenced reply
but instead you launched
into a lecture
on the properties of yttrium
or something
and I just nodded along
in case I nodded off.
"Tree huggers at one o'clock," you said.
"The Ladyboys of Bangkok," I said.
A lone oak holding onto its leaves.
The present is always
the best time to be alive
but even The Garden of Eden has weeds.

## I Sometimes Forget

Being neighbourly nowadays
is on point and very trendy
but I find that lad who works in the Co-op
to be somewhat over-friendly.
So what if I get confused
between Neil Diamond and Neil Sedaka
and I sometimes forget
before I order it
that I don't like moussaka.
You see aubergines are not my thing
but I do like to binge
on my tv box sets
(Who's the one who sang *Sweet Caroline*?)
over nibbles
and a glass of red wine.
I make critiques of them all
I've noted how the theme tune ends abruptly
at the start of *Better Call Saul*.

Robbing from the rich
has been enshrined in the law
because nowadays there's nothing left
to steal from the poor.
So what if I get confused
between Adolf Hitler and Margaret Thatcher
and I sometimes forget
before I write a killer poem
that they're hard to manufacture.
You see being a genius is not me
but I do like to binge
on my tv box sets
(Who dropped more bombs on my city?)
over nibbles
and something pretty
I make critiques and write them all down.
I've noted the high production values
in period dramas like *The Crown*.

## Dick

Dick plies his trade, alfresco,
taking a job at the local Tesco
shunting discarded supermarket trollies
seeking opportunities to get his jollies.

He follows the racing from Uttoxeter
cos he likes a bet and a beer
but in the 3:45, his horse, *Double Entendre*
is bringing up the rear.
"Ooer missus
that's a whopper!"
He's indulging in risque chit chat
with the lady who's a mystery shopper.

He enjoys a round of innuendo bingo
with that redhead who drives the Renault Twingo
and he loves a bit of saucy banter
with her, the one in the Seat Alhambra.

But the drinks will flow tonight for Dick
for him there'll be joy unconfined
'cos in the 3:45, his horse, *Double Entendre*
has only come from behind.
"Ooer missus
titter ye not!"
He's indulging in ribald dialogue
with the ladies in the parking lot.

## While You Went

While you went yomping in the Cotswolds
staying in cheap and dirty youth hostels
wistfully expanding your personal experience
at the cost of an underwhelming ambience;
I was a trawlerman hauling an empty catch
trying to strike a light with a damp match
ready to dash when the traffic lights flashed amber
always the moronic, brain-dead gambler.

While you went whale watching in the Inner Hebrides;
I was picking strawberries down on my knees
and railing against the social inequity
flailing against the global iniquity
but I'm out of here, get me a celebrity,
someone with some fucking integrity
because this clinically deficient dissident
is telling you a management decision's imminent.

While you went riding astride your white stallion
with that hairy-arsed ape and his medallion;
I saw that you were just a phase I went through
but a man's gotta do and paddle his own canoe.
It's time I kicked over those dying embers
and jumped your ship, and tried to remember
to play no more the pandering protagonist
to your glib philandering narcissist.

While you went flagellating my spiny back;
I think I decided to give you the sack.
Take a look around at all that I fought
after playing around with irrational thought.
Now golden syrup coats my wooden spoon
and up there shines another supermoon
cut me some cheese and butter me a bap
go shuffle the deck and fetch me my cap.

## Phil

Here he comes now
his life in abeyance
smoothing down the tarmac
in his motorised conveyance.
England's botox-faced glory
can't work now he's too ill.
Let me tell you the story
of my childhood mate Phil.

Once active on the poetry scene
he liked a bit of the spoken word.
Didn't do owt mucky or obscene
had a bit of a taste for the absurd
went in for political satire
targeting the Tories and Donald Trump
expressing his scorn and his ire
but now he's defeated
and sat on his rump.

Ah yes Philip
twin-batteried commuter
neutered and rooted to his chair
and to be fair
when I look at him
there's a twinge
of guilt and remorse.
I admit there's a cringe
a regret of sorts.
But I do feel better
since I bought him his scooter
in the January sales.
It was the least I could do
for pushing him off that mountain
in North Wales.

We were lifetime friends after all.
Not that it counted for much

when I stood and watched him fall
after giving him a gentle nudge.
We first became mates at school
went to punk gigs together.
We were the epitome of cool
in our tartan and our leather.
We stumbled upon the work
of John Cooper Clarke
and the rest as they say is history
a wordsmith's inspirational spark
exploring life's mysteries.

We got active on the poetry scene
we liked a bit of the spoken word.
Didn't do owt mucky or obscene
had a bit of a taste for the absurd
went in for political satire
targeting the Tories and Maggie Thatcher
expressing our scorn and our ire
we'd never be defeated
by the infamous milk-snatcher.

But at the mic from time to time
Phil got right on my tits
with his propensity to force a rhyme
with lines that just didn't fit.
You may think me a tad harsh
for taking such a stance
that appeared somewhat intransigent
but I saw my opportunity
I took my chance
and I made it look like an accident.
He wrote one about the Sex Pistols
and that famous interview they did
where he tried to rhyme Bill Grundy
(via a spurious reference to Hereford Cathedral)
with the Mappa Mundi.
Further on in that poem
he even tried to rhyme 'seditious'

yeah, with young Sidney
the bass player
who's viciously no longer with us.

He's forgiven me now for putting him
in a state of catatonia
after all what happens in North Wales
stays in Snowdonia.
But if he ever gets up on that stage again
I'm not liable for my actions.
For him it's gonna be Armageddon
and the rest of his life in traction.
We used to be the best of mates
but he tipped me over the edge
with rhymes so bad they used to grate
until I shoved him off that Welsh ledge.

Ah yes Philip the twin-batteried commuter
neutered and rooted to his chair
and to be fair
when I look at him
there's a twinge
of guilt and remorse.
I admit there's a cringe
a regret of sorts.
And that's the sad tale
of my erstwhile pal
that I thought you ought'a know.
His life changed direction
with a little deflection
off a clifftop in Llandudno.

## Norman and Shirley and Me

I was in a restaurant with my friends Norman and Shirley.
It was November, and the restaurant
had the Christmas decorations up.
Shirley moaned about it, as usual.
Shirley always moans about people getting into Christmas too early.
Norman always moans about Shirley moaning about Christmas
and I can't stand moaners who moan
about people's moaning about Christmas.
I always moan about their constant moaning.
I guess that makes me as bad as them.

And then the waiter came over to take the order.
Norman wanted to know the extent
to which all the items on the menu
contained gluten, lactose or traces of nut.
Norman's got all the food intolerances.
Shirley's always intolerant of Norman's intolerances
and I can't stand intolerant types
being intolerant of people's food intolerances.
I'm always intolerant of their lack of tolerance.
I guess that makes me as bad as them.

At the end of the meal we couldn't decide how to pay.
I asked for individual bills,
so we could all pay for our own food.
Shirley moaned, and Norman couldn't tolerate the idea.
They always complained about the bill not being split equally.
I always complain about their complaints.
And Norman and Shirley can't stand complainants
complaining about people's complaints.
They always complain about complainers.
I guess that makes them as bad as me.

It was cold outside, and we tried to flag down a taxi.
The streets were full of homeless people
freezing in the rain.
It was intolerable, and we moaned and complained

about having a good night out ruined.
We always have to step over and around homeless people.
We can't stand having to step over and around
homeless people freezing in the rain.
They always ruin a good night out.
I guess that makes them as bad as us.

## Games Night

Garret window framing a planetary eclipse
seeking mediocrity in passing ships.
A starburst, bobbing-head chameleon,
an eagle-eyed, misguided authoritarian,
handlebar-moustache, tailor made
florid complexion, goose the chambermaid
and making a shifty, makeshift observatory;
it's Colonel Mustard, in the conservatory
bashing that head with undue ceremony
holistic missile, ballistic therapy.

And all the while seeking fellowship with
an overwatered peace lily and the remnants
of a takeaway Rogan josh.

Clotted cream and Neolithic burial mounds,
megaliths and ley lines over holy ground.
A chunk of blue labradorite,
an unidentified piece of chlorite,
whistle-stop, bling-ring fundraiser,
wishful-thinking, navel gazer
and every inch the sodden, downtrodden maverick;
it's Reverend Green with the candlestick
mangling the hallowed oesophagus
jangling the keys to your sarcophagus.

And all the while seeking fellowship with
an overwatered peace lily and the remnants
of a takeaway Rogan josh.

Freight train, needlepoint ballet dancer,
smokescreen, querulous, fingertip chancer.
A fragrant, polytheistic, stylistic mystic,
a slash of slut red lipstick,
stinging jellyfish tentacles,
nettlebed thrumming ventricles
and listening to the strains of Gustav Mahler;

it's Miss Scarlett, with the revolver
pumping your belly full of lead
until you're deader than the deadest of the dead.

And all the while seeking fellowship with
an overwatered peace lily and the remnants
of a takeaway Rogan josh.

## Uncle Mike

"Pall bearers ready!"
We stand, lined up
then in unison
we lift carefully
three of us on the left.
Each of us settles
the great weight
onto a shoulder
three of us on the right
and carefully we turn
towards the congregation.

I was seven years old
when you came to the house
on your push bike.
I expressed my fascination
and you asked me if I wanted
to go for a ride.
You lifted me over the crossbar
and climbed onto the saddle
securing me between
those powerful forearms
as you reached for the handlebars.

Through the back-yard door
we went
into the alleyway
and out onto cobbles
your enormous strength
and skill
keeping us upright
and all I had to do
was be
as we cut through
the lead grey of Anfield.

How odd that we journeyed

in silence.

My mind hurries back now
to that childhood memory.
I'm returning the favour.
I carry you
as you once carried me.
I'm the strong one
keeping us upright
and all you have to do
is be
as we cut through
the lead grey of the church.

How odd that we journey
in silence.

## Crouch and Await Your Turn

Witness the levelling cataclysm arrive.
Who do you suppose is going to survive?
It's not the complacent idle rich.
It's those who know how to dig a ditch,
skin rabbits, find water, make fire
amid that barbaric holy choir.
Warping glassy-eyed hallucination.
Havoc-wreaked malignant temptation.

When the world's a deconstruction site
with no communication satellites
and all we hear is *Radio Ga Ga*
twisted lips chant hallelujah!
Never quite what you would expect,
the Mercury in retrograde effect.

The patience and guile of lunar beats.
Golden spurs wrapped round our feet.
Within each of us a God-like state
banishes fear that manifests as hate.
Try not to die in Cirencester
on this the last Sunday of summer.
Our turn at last to leave the hives
end this agreement to fake our own lives.

When the world's a deconstruction site
with no communication satellites
and all we hear is *Radio Ga Ga*
twisted lips chant hallelujah!
Never quite what you would expect,
the Mercury in retrograde effect.

We are wheat for the harvesting breeze
curved and bent fit to appease.
That hard-won memorised catechism
no match for the new-found liberalism
of perception now recalibrated.

The divinity of Nature celebrated.
On stone our egos ground and milled.
Pregnant soils freshly tilled.

When the world's a deconstruction site
with no communication satellites
and all we hear is *Radio Ga Ga*
twisted lips chant hallelujah!
Never quite what you would expect,
the Mercury in retrograde effect.

## Hilton Park Services

In a motorway service station off the M6
I parked my car because I needed a piss
and while I was at it, a cup of tea
better make that a cake, a cuppa and a pee.

I shoved through the heaving throng of humanity
through travellers disrobed of individuality
into a plastic world of corporate brands
harvesting our base demands.

A fake, rustic, soul sucking oxymora
"I'm here to serve, my name's Laura."
It held no attraction, I felt no reverie
towards this financially ruinous bonhomie.

So, I gave the toilet visit sole priority
whilst trying to ignore the awful sonority
of Christmas songs in fucking November.
You can count me out, I'm a non-member.

Motorway service station restaurant
perhaps there's no greater testament.
The national malaise that always unnerves.
We get the service stations we deserve.

I decided to swerve the bill of fayre
the air smelt so much sweeter out of there
and over the southbound carriageway
a murmuration of starlings showed me the way.

## Mighty Silver

A ramrod streak tears across
a blue, canvas sky
and with a mighty silver roar
bellows its beauty from high.

Metallic heart of aluminium
jet propelled fuselage
pulsed with electricity
that flying bird visage.

I watch from where I stand
those dead wings fixed in flight
at boiling white tail feathers
and try as I might

I cannot move my eyes
from the miracle I seek
that distant bird above
mighty silver, ramrod streak

## The 13:45

I'm forced to turn sharply
by a speeding truck
and I knock my left wing mirror off
in a hedge.
I can now enjoy the rest of my trip
without worrying about
knocking my left wing mirror off
in a hedge
because it's already off.

Then a passenger tells me she's just had a haircut.
I try to tell her that it looks nice
without sounding creepy,
but I fail.
I say the haircut looks nice
and I sound creepy.

But I don't know if I'm too creepy
or if I'm not creepy enough.
I just know I can't put up with
this rigmarole any more
with all the malarkey and chicanery.

I'll shortly be going into hospital
for an operation to fix
a symptom of my new,
stress related illness.
I can now enjoy the rest of my trip
without worrying about
developing a
stress related illness
because I've already got one.

Then a man in a dress shows me his new tattoo.
I try to tell him that the tattoo is cool
without sounding fake
but I fail.

I say the tattoo is cool
and I sound fake.

But I don't know if I'm too fake
or if I'm not fake enough.
I just know I can't put up with
this palaver any more
with all the hocus-pocus and mumbo-jumbo.

Bus drivers don't have seatbelts
because we're not deemed worthy
so when I crash and fly
through the windscreen
I'll be able to enjoy the rest of my trip
without worrying about
crashing the bus and flying
through the windscreen
because I'll have already crashed.

Then a kid gives me a half-sucked lollipop.
I try to force a smile and say thank-you
without sounding insincere
but I fail.
I force a smile and say thank-you
and I sound insincere.

But I don't know if I'm too insincere
or if I'm not insincere enough.
I just know I can't put up with
these shenanigans any more
with all the flim-flam
and the claptrap
with the poppycock
and the balderdash
and the jiggery-pokery

with all the gobbledygook
and all that skulduggery.

## The Song of the Whale

Discarded petals and paper packets
dress the leaves that the spider plant spun.
All hail the painting on the paperback jacket,
it's Rembrandt's *Return of the Prodigal Son*.

This lyrical life is strangely inferior
and embraces all that I've loathed
but the truth beneath my naked exterior
is I've always remained fully clothed.

Listen in trust to the song of the whale
though you may not be that type of poet.
We all supped in unison from the Holy Grail
but not all of us were given to show it.

Cosmic Microwave Background hiss
to the dance of the four-leafed clover.
I can see some people are on the piss
as they think the pandemic's all over.

Prophets have said not to have such concerns
yet it's clear we've never understood.
We can't take our poverty with us
though we seem to wish that we could.

## Brexit Indifference

Duality, pole shifted.

Half-evolution, part convolution
I remember it now
a flashback to that backlash
that dash back to the haberdashery
a slapdash whiplash,
thrash trash, backslash common market
backwash whitewash
white water rafting
at the hands of your gondolier
shredded nerves hanging from a chandelier
of cracked glass splitting light
with a thousand prisms.

Duality, pole shifted.

Gripped with terror
wrists limp and hanging
dangling into negative space
monocultural sobriety
of cavernous insignificance
harmony, distortion, disharmony
torn bioluminescent skin
flecked and textured hollow chest
burgers and chips
burgers and chips
monetary union
synchronicity.

Duality, pole shifted.

## Listening to Claude Debussy

If music is the space between notes
then life is the breath between long deaths
where fractured light silhouettes your soul.
Tremulous fingers tremblingly point me to the prison
though I'm not committed enough to finish my sentence.
I'm all half-hearted; hesitant like winter sleet
uniformly uninformed with manufactured hope
wintry showers and plastic bags on the street.

Already it's Thursday afternoon
and I'm listening to Claude Debussy.
There are pigeons on my roof.
Rat-a-tat-tat, clackety-clack.

If music is the space between notes
then poetry is the silence between long stanzas
where braided rivers replenish your soul.
Limitless grandeur unlimited has a trajectory
though I'm not blessed with a persistence of vision.
I'm all half-hearted; a jocular troubadour
a rumbling tumble of manufactured dope
with all the chintz of a second-rate raconteur.

Already it's Thursday afternoon
and I'm listening to Claude Debussy.
There are pigeons on my roof.
Rat-a-tat-tat, clackety-clack.
Rat-a-tat-tat, clackety-clack.

Rat-a-tat-tat, clackety-clack.

# Prick

A model of deflection
following the gods of reason blindly on.
Not intelligent enough to ignore the science.
Lacking the requisite imagination.
Paying no heed to the voices at night.
Too cynical to entertain them.
No brains left in that tool overnight.
No masterpiece of creation then.
Instead a pen and paper sniper
a belly-crawling, forked-tongued griper
inconspicuous viper.
If I'm a prick,
me,
do I not bleed?

Memories that scar.
Joining the Party-Til-You-Puke party.
Not brave enough to waft a wonderful wand.
Lacking the requisite wit and wisdom.
The smell of overweight mongrel.
Upswell of uprisen jealousy.
A sourpuss of unsurpassed doggerel.
No masterpiece of creation this.
Believing in nothing but empty space.
All solid matter disappeared without grace
inconspicuous trace.
If I'm a prick,
me,
do I not bleed?

## I've Never Been to Bletchley

I've never been to Bletchley.
I've never wanted to, especially
but perhaps while you're there
you'll discover
the next Elvis Presley?

Just because you read stuff on the Internet
doesn't mean that it's false
if your inner voice tells you to listen
in Bletchley.

Just because it doesn't come easily
doesn't mean that it's hard
if you give yourself permission
in Bletchley.

I've never been to Bletchley.
I've never wanted to, especially
but perhaps while you're there
you'll uncover
a long-lost Botticelli?

Just because you're not travelling fast
doesn't mean you're standing still
if you shift your position
in Bletchley.

Just because you're away from home
doesn't mean that you're lost
if you trust your intuition
in Bletchley.

And now I have been to Bletchley
to visit you, twice to be precise
but finally, once there
I understood
why you think it's not so nice.

## Daisyworld

Daisyworld has black daisies.
Daisyworld has white daisies.
Black daisies absorb the light
and warm Daisyworld.
White daises reflect the light
and cool Daisyworld.
A balanced equilibrium
between black daisies
and white daisies
leads to a Daisyworld
where temperature is optimal
for daisy growth.

## Breakfast at Erol's

A full English with a rack of toast
or some fancy baguette
courtesy of mine host
a mushroom omelette
all suspicious activity
breakfast at Erol's
CCTV in operation
cholesterol poisoning
but only in moderation
all suspicious activity
breakfast at Erol's
all suspicious activity
breakfast at Erol's
all suspicious activity will be reported.

We're face to face not Skyped
sanitized not wiped
all suspicious activity
breakfast at Erol's
all suspicious activity will be reported to the police
all suspicious activity
breakfast at Erol's
all suspicious activity
breakfast at Erol's
all suspicious activity will be reported to the police and other retailers.

We do track and trace
and some fancy baguette
keep your distancing space
a dash of vinaigrette
all tables and chairs
breakfast at Erol's
we've got outdoor seating
cholesterol poisoning
but please ignore the sleeting
all tables and chairs

breakfast at Erol's
all tables and chairs
breakfast at Erol's
all tables and chairs are fully sanitized.

We're face to face not Skyped
sanitized not wiped
all tables and chairs
breakfast at Erol's
all tables and chairs are fully sanitized before and after use
all tables and chairs
breakfast at Erol's
all tables and chairs
breakfast at Erol's
all tables and chairs are fully sanitized before and after use for your own safety.

Breakfast at Erol's
all suspicious activity
breakfast at Erol's
all tables and chairs
breakfast at Erol's
all suspicious activity
breakfast at Erol's
all tables and chairs.

...At the embalmed village of St Weonards
a wooden road sign informs
and I make mental notes.
234 miles to Lands End
six twenty-nine John O'Groats.

*From 'Drizzle over Hereford' (page 28)*

Derek Dohren has been performing his poetry on the spoken word circuit in England's south-west since October 2017. He has been described as "quirky and surreal"; as "a shark basking in a sea of words"; and as a poet who enjoys rooting out "affectation and pomposity".

More prosaically he is a bus driver, the latest profession from which he draws artistic inspiration.

# Other Works by Derek Dohren

His first poetry collection, 'Everything Rhymes with Orange' was published by Black Eyes Publishing UK in July 2019

ISBN-13 978-1913195038


## Reviews: 'Everything Rhymes with Orange'

**A C Jackson:** Within this collection of 31 poems you have, sadness, wry humour, regret, "what the hell is going on?", laugh-out-loud humour, observations on quirky behaviour, quirky observations on everyday stuff, fantasy and surreal happenings. I will read many of these poems many times more.

**Pelagia Pais:** Derek's poetry makes me smile. It is clever, humorous, it has a sort of a rhythm. There are poems that feel like they have both real life and pure imagination intertwined. Others that show the traps of the overthinking mind. Some are deep and emotional, others are playful. I would urge you to buy this book. You won't regret it. I also invite you to go and watch Derek perform live where he brings individuality and charisma.

**Edith Ryan:**  The quirkiness of the cover and the title caught my eye and the more of the poems I read the more i wanted to read on, smiling here, nodding there and warming to the writing. I could imagine it read aloud. Some of the sharpness of the observations required a second reading and i will go on reading them.

**Roger Hare:**  Derek gives us words from his heart to ours - there's no ballast here, just gemstone observations and considerations borne of real life......., something for everyone :)

**Jennie Farley:**  Derek Dohren tells his stories with warmth and humour, and a modicum of self-deprecation which adds to the charm of the collection. Taking a walk with an imaginary dog, sitting in cafés people-watching, living a pretend-life as 'Martin' ... these poems are too edgy to be entirely whimsical, to poignant to be trivial. This poet captures profound moments in the everyday imbued with his own particular form of philosophy.
A joy to read!

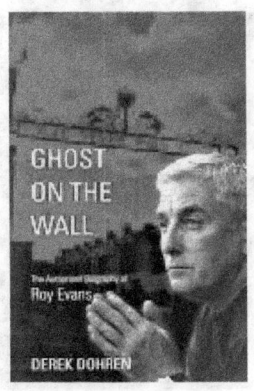

Ghost on the Wall (Mainstream Publishing)
ISBN-13 978-1840188325, published 2004.

The authorised biography of former Liverpool FC player and manager Roy Evans.

*"Now the move has failed and the board has decided to get back to basics. It is determined to turn back the clock. But is it too late? The Kop holds its collective breath. Roy Evans, the last of the Boot Room boys, steps forward to keep his date with destiny."*

"... Dohren's book is a well-written reappraisal of Evans."
**FourFourTwo magazine**

"How many times have you clicked on a promising title only to find either rehashed 'news' items or else some piece of complete drivel? Fortunately, there are still some writers you can rely on. Derek Dohren is one of them."
**Paul Grech, Walk On web site, walkonlfc.com**

"It's the insightful chapters that cover his management years that will most demand the attention of Liverpool fans."
**liverpoolfc.tv, Official club web site**

"I am a big fan of biographies and this one was superb."
**Ian Coumbe, Bromborough**

The Cats of the River Darro (CreateSpace Publishing)
ISBN-13 978-1478315537, published 2012.

A semi-autobiographical account of a broken life being rebuilt in the charming shadow of Granada's Alhambra Palace, beautifully illustrated by artist Natasha Phillips.

"I have come across the work of mathematician Doron Zeilberger. Rather splendidly he is of the opinion that there is no such thing as infinity. He wonderfully said of it, *"I don't think I ever liked it. I always found something repulsive about it."*

\* \* \*

Awarded Landscape Artist of the Year 2009 by Artists and Illustrators Magazine for his painting
**'The Fossil Hunters'**

Derek's artwork can be viewed at
**www.derekdohren.com**